Biblical Counseling Foundation (BCF)

LIVING VICTORIOUSLY IN THE BATTLES OF LIFE

This booklet is published by the Biblical Counseling Foundation, Inc., a non-profit, non-stock corporation founded in 1974 and incorporated in the Commonwealth of Virginia, USA, in 1977.

The material is excerpted and adapted from the Biblical Counseling Foundation's 480 page in-depth discipleship manual titled, **Self-Confrontation** (1991 edition) and the associated **Student Workbook**.

Copyright: The contents of this booklet are copyrighted © 2010 and 2012 by the Biblical Counseling Foundation, Inc. All rights reserved. Reproduction in any manner in whole or in part, in English and/or other languages, or storage in a retrieval system, or transmission in any form or by any means — electronic, mechanical, visual, audio, or any other — except for brief quotations in printed reviews is prohibited without written permission of the Biblical Counseling Foundation (BCF).

Scripture taken from the New American Standard Bible, © 1960, 1962, 1963, 1968, 1971, 1972, 1973, 1975, 1977 by The Lockman Foundation. Used by permission.

ISBN 978-1-60536-040-9

First printing, September, 2010, printed in Hong Kong
Second printing, July, 2012, printed in Hong Kong

Biblical Counseling Foundation
42550 Aegean Street
Indio, CA 92203-9617, USA

760.347.4608 telephone
760.775.5751 fax
orders@bcfministries.org e-mail for orders
admin@bcfministries.org e-mail for other
877.933.9333 (in USA) telephone for orders only
www.bcfministries.org webpage for orders and information

2

© BIBLICAL COUNSELING FOUNDATION

TABLE OF CONTENTS

	content	page
Introduction	Why This Study?	5
Lesson 1	Getting Started in Your Faith	7
Lesson 2	What Does the Bible Say about Tests, Temptations, and Problems?	13
Lesson 3	The Downward Spiral of Defeat	19
Lesson 4	Biblical Hope	25
Lesson 5	Biblical Change: Dealing with Problems God's Way	31
Lesson 6	Biblical Practice: Your Daily Walk with Christ	37

Supplements

Supplement 1	Where to Find Biblical References to Specific Problem Areas	43
Supplement 2	Bible Study and Application Format	45
Supplement 3	Answers to Questions in the Booklet	47

© BIBLICAL COUNSELING FOUNDATION

4

© BIBLICAL COUNSELING FOUNDATION

INTRODUCTION

WHY THIS STUDY?

Living Victoriously in the Battles of Life is a life-application Bible study about how Christians can be victorious in the daily battles and struggles of life. The study can be used in conjunction with or in follow-up to other Bible studies that focus on Christian growth and discipleship. Its purpose is to help equip believers to face, deal with, and endure the tests and temptations of life, in the power of the Holy Spirit. Although this study is designed for use by even new believers, all believers will benefit from it.

Tests and temptations do not go away once we become a believer. In fact, problems may even intensify. God, in His love, continues to use trials to help us grow and mature spiritually – to take in the "solid food" of His Word *(Hebrews 5:14)*. God provides great hope and instruction for us in His Word about living victoriously even when life is difficult. The spiritual fruit of this study will come by both learning these principles and by putting them into practice.

This study can be used in several ways:

- In your own personal devotions and Bible study;
- To help a friend by going through the biblical principles together; or
- As a small group Bible study or Sunday school class.

There is a great contrast between man's way and God's way of dealing with problems. God says in *Isaiah 55:8-9* that His ways are much higher than our ways. *Verse 11* describes the power of God's Word to accomplish His purposes. We will see in this study that the difference between the world's view and God's truth is dramatic, and God has provided some tremendous resources for us to be overwhelming conquerors over our problems, even when there appears to be little hope.

The study covers the following topics:

Lesson 1: Getting started in your faith;

Lesson 2: What does the Bible say about tests, temptations, and problems?;

Lesson 3: The downward spiral of defeat;

Lesson 4: Biblical hope;

Lesson 5: Biblical change: dealing with problems God's way; and

Lesson 6: Biblical practice: your daily walk with Christ.

God has much more practical guidance in His Word about facing, dealing with, and enduring the trials of life than many Christians realize. This study will help you learn and apply these principles and prepare you to help others. As you go through this study, you will see that there are questions, Bible passages to look up, and spaces for you to fill in the answers. If you are not sure of some of the answers, you can look up the answers for most questions in the back of this booklet. Just refer to the corresponding lesson number and question number. If you are going through this study as a group, your group leader may be able to help you as well. You can do part of a lesson each day until you're done.

If you are going through the study on your own, you can go at your own pace. The lessons are designed so that you can go through them in a week with no more than about 15 minutes per day.

© BIBLICAL COUNSELING FOUNDATION

INTRODUCTION

WHY THIS STUDY?

Some lessons are a little longer than others. But you can do more or less, depending on the time you have. This is meant to get you started in a life-long practice of studying the Word of God on a regular basis. May the Lord bless you as you learn and apply His Word.

LESSON 1

GETTING STARTED IN YOUR FAITH

This short-course is about Christians living victoriously in the daily battles and struggles of life. It is also about how to come alongside others and help them through those challenging times. This training shows believers how to become firmly grounded in their faith and to demonstrate the fruit of the Spirit *(Galatians 5:22, 23)* in even the most difficult of circumstances. This is supernatural living, and it would not be possible without the resources that the Lord has provided to us as believers. This course will help you learn what those resources are, how to apply them in overcoming the daily problems of life, and how to encourage others to do the same.

Jesus was very specific with His disciples about the challenges of life. He didn't tell the disciples that their problems would go away if they followed Him. Instead, He warned them that difficult times would come, and He prepared them for the battles they would face as His followers. He told them what they would face, showed them how to deal victoriously with those trials, and was Himself the ultimate demonstration of victorious living.

But before beginning our study of the battles of life and how to live victoriously in them, we need to make sure we are all starting on a solid foundation. You may be very familiar with these fundamentals of the Christian life, but it is always good to go back through them again. This foundation is critical for all believers, both young and old in the Lord.

Becoming a believer in Jesus Christ is the greatest and most life-changing decision a person can make. If you have made that decision, you have been born into God's family. Just as in a physical family, a new member of God's spiritual family should expect to grow. This lesson is about several important areas of your Christian life: reading the Bible (God's communication to us), assurance of your salvation, the Holy Spirit, prayer (our communication with God), fellowship with other believers, and committing God's Word to memory.

A. The Bible

God has revealed Himself to you through the Bible, and reading the Bible is one of the main ways you can get to know Him. You will be amazed at how practical the Bible is for your life today, even though it was written several thousand years ago.

Even if you are not familiar with the Bible, with a little direction you can find your way around easily. Each of the books of the Bible is divided into "chapters" and "verses." You can locate a book of the Bible by going to the table of contents near the front to find the page where each book starts. Frequently, There are two lists of books in the table of contents, one for the Old Testament and one for the New Testament. So when we refer to *John 3:16,* for example, that just means the Gospel according to John (in the New Testament), Chapter 3, Verse 16. So let's get started.

Read *John 20:30-31.* What was God's purpose for you in directing John to write down the events in his Gospel?

1.

© BIBLICAL COUNSELING FOUNDATION

LESSON 1

GETTING STARTED IN YOUR FAITH

The Gospel of John and the other three Gospels (Matthew, Mark, and Luke) all contain historical facts about the Lord Jesus, His teaching and commands, and His ministry on earth. These were recorded so that our faith in Christ might be increased and so that we might follow Him. In fact, the entire Bible is written to build us up and give us direction for living.

Read *II Timothy 3:16-17.* What does the first part of *verse 16* say about God's Word?

2. _____

The whole Bible is "inspired" or "God-breathed." What we are reading in the Bible is God's Word, not merely man's sayings or philosophies. God used men to write the words down for us to read today. Also in *verse 16,* what four things are the Scriptures profitable for?

3. _____

In other words, the Bible is a practical guide to help us in our daily lives as Christians.

God's Word teaches us how to show love to God and others. As a mirror shows what is lacking, God's Word also reproves us when we fail to demonstrate love. As we are corrected, the Bible shows us what to do in place of our failure. Finally, the Bible trains us as we make and fulfill specific plans for right living.

And what is the end result, in *verse 17?*

4. _____

We are to be prepared for the opportunities God gives us to show our love for Him and others. This whole study focuses on how to draw from the Scriptures hope and practical guidance for the daily battles we face as believers. Lesson 6 has specific information about how to get to know God through study and application of His Word.

B. Assurance of your salvation

Your salvation is based on the promises of God. Read *John 5:24.* What does your eternal life depend on?

5. _____

_____

It is wonderful to know that eternal life with Christ does not depend on how good we have been or how we feel. Our feelings may come and go, but our salvation is based on the promise of God that the penalty for our sin has been paid through the death of Jesus Christ on the cross. Then He rose from the dead to demonstrate God's power over death. What does *Romans 6:23* say about eternal life?

6. _____

_____

Eternal life is a free gift. There is no way that we deserve this intimate relationship with Christ, nor can we earn it. Also, He promises in *Hebrews 13:5* that He will never desert us nor forsake us. We should spend the rest of our lives thanking God for His mercy and grace by living in the

© BIBLICAL COUNSELING FOUNDATION

LESSON 1

GETTING STARTED IN YOUR FAITH

way He guides us to live. This is reinforced in *Ephesians 2:8-9*. How does this passage say we are saved?

7. _____

_____

In *verse 10,* you can see that God has even prepared good works for you to do, but your deeds do not earn salvation.

Why don't you pause right now and thank Him for providing you with the gift of eternal life. If you are unsure of your salvation, or have not yet accepted that gift, consider reviewing some additional passages such as *Romans 3:23, Romans 5:8, Romans 10:9-10,* and *Romans 10:13.*

God says in *Romans 10:9* that when you believe in Jesus, you confess Him as your Lord (which also means "Master"). This is a public declaration that Jesus is now Lord of your life. You are to submit to Him as your Master or Head. You are placing yourself under His management. We do not accept Jesus as Savior one day and determine whether we will accept Him as Lord later on. Both of these are part of the same decision we make to invite Jesus Christ into our lives as our Master.

At this point, begin memorizing *Ephesians 2:8-9.* You will receive information on the importance of Scripture memory in Section F. of this lesson.

C. The Holy Spirit

Shortly before He died on the cross, Jesus told His followers that He would be going away but that God would also leave them with a Helper, the Holy Spirit. Read *John 14:26* and *John 16:13.* What do these verses say the Holy Spirit will help you with?

8. _____

_____

The Holy Spirit will teach you and help you with the understanding of the Word of God. What else does the Holy Spirit do according to *Romans 5:5?*

9. _____

The Holy Spirit dwells within you, if you are a believer in Christ. God poured out His love on you when you were saved, and from then on you have a new power to love others, in a way you never could before.

D. Prayer

Prayer is simply talking with God. We can pray out loud or silently, by ourselves or with others. We tend to think about prayer mainly when we think we need God's help in some way. But prayer is also a matter of praising and thanking God, and sometimes confessing our sin so that we can be restored to fellowship with Him. What does God say in *Psalm 116:1-2?*

10. _____

_____

© BIBLICAL COUNSELING FOUNDATION

LESSON 1

GETTING STARTED IN YOUR FAITH

When we talk to God, we know that He is listening. But there is something that can get in the way of our communication with God. What is that according to *Psalm 66:18?*

11. _____

We need to go to God in prayer without harboring (cherishing or holding on to) sin in our heart. When we as believers commit sin, this grieves the Holy Spirit, but it does not alter our family relationship with God. We are still called His children. But it does affect our fellowship (unhindered communication or communion) with Him. What does God say in *I John 1:9* that we need to do to restore our fellowship with God?

12. _____

Confess means to agree with God that you have not followed His commands as you should have. You are also saying that your intent is not to sin in that way again. In that same verse, what is God's promise if you confess your sins?

13. _____

You can be completely confident in His faithfulness to forgive you.

E. Fellowship with other believers

The church is called the "body of Christ," and individual believers, including you, are members of that body. Read *I Corinthians 12:25-27.* What does *verse 26* say you do as a member of the body of Christ?

14. _____

Not only do we rejoice and sometimes suffer together, but God says that you are to care for other members of the body. Being in the body of Christ is like an extended family. It is a great privilege, but also carries with it some responsibilities. Read *Hebrews 10:24-25.* What are some of the things God says you should be doing with others in the body of Christ?

15. _____

Believers need to gather together on a regular basis to stimulate one another to action, both inside and outside the church. God instructs you to get involved in a local body of believers, if you have not already done so. It is important for you, and it is important for them as well.

LESSON 1

GETTING STARTED IN YOUR FAITH

F. Scripture memory

God says in *Romans 12:2* that we are not to be *16.* _____

to the world but to be *17.* _____

by the renewing of our mind.

We need to cooperate with God, doing His will, and as He transforms us we will experience His good and perfect will. We don't normally carry a Bible with us every minute of the day, but we can take God's Word with us in our mind. The Holy Spirit can then use our recollection of the Scriptures we know to help us with moment-by-moment choices and decisions. An important habit to begin as a Christian is to start memorizing portions of Scripture that can help us through the day. It takes effort to establish this habit, but it can have tremendous benefits in your life.

Read *Psalm 119:9, 11.* What benefits are there to treasuring God's Word in your heart and obeying it completely?

18. _____

_____

11

It is important for you to have a specific plan for memorizing God's Word, starting with verses that apply directly to your life in your current situation. For example, if you are tempted to worry, memorize *Matthew 6:25* and some of the verses that follow. Or if you are dealing with anger, consider memorizing *James 1:19-20.*

A lot of people are concerned that they are not good at memorizing and don't have enough time for it. Yes, it does require repetition, and it will take some time. But think about all the times and places in which you can make wise use of your time by memorizing at the same time you are doing other things that do not require much detailed thinking – while washing dishes or standing in line at the bank, for example. All you need is to have some verses written down on cards and keep them with you or put them in the right place. So take advantage of these moments during the day. List some possible times during the day that might be possibilities for you to memorize Scripture.

19. _____

_____

This *Living Victoriously* Bible study provides a verse or verses for you to memorize as you study each lesson. Before each lesson, whether you are studying by yourself or with a group, recite the verse to someone else, so that he or she can help you get it right, word for word.

G. What was the most significant truth you learned in completing this lesson?

20. _____

_____

© BIBLICAL COUNSELING FOUNDATION

LESSON 1

GETTING STARTED IN YOUR FAITH

H. For the next lesson:

1. If you have not already recited *Ephesians 2:8-9,* be sure to ask someone to check you as you recite the passage.

2. Begin memorizing *I Peter 4:12* and prepare to recite this passage for the next lesson.

3. Study all of Lesson 2 and answer the questions. Do a little bit of the lesson each day.

4. Check your answers in the back of the booklet.

Lesson 2 teaches that our problems do not go away once we become a Christian. However, we have new resources that we did not have before, enabling us to live victoriously in every situation. As you start Lesson 2, think of it as part of developing the habit of daily devotions.

12

© BIBLICAL COUNSELING FOUNDATION

LESSON 2

WHAT DOES THE BIBLE SAY ABOUT TESTS, TEMPTATIONS, AND PROBLEMS?

Before you begin this lesson, ask for God's help in understanding His Word and for wisdom and strength to apply what you learn in the power of the Holy Spirit.

Begin memorizing *I Peter 4:12* and prepare to recite this passage before the next lesson.

Jesus gave us His plan for reaching the world through being and making disciples. Read the "Great Commission" passage in *Matthew 28:19-20.* What are the two parts to this commandment?

1. _____

Jesus said that we are both to baptize (with evangelism implied) and to teach or train others. Telling others about the Gospel is the way believers reach the world, and is included as the first part of making disciples. The second part is to train believers to live victoriously, that is "teaching them to observe" *all* that He commanded.

To see some of what He commanded, scan through the topics Jesus dealt with in the Sermon on the Mount *(Matthew Chapters 5 - 7).* He talked about how to face and deal with anger, persecution, reconciliation, lustful temptations, relationship problems, retaliation, divorce, hatred, and worry, among others. He prepared His disciples to deal with and endure the problems of life, knowing that these problems could discourage them or sidetrack them from their mission.

These are examples of the "battles of life" that we still experience today. People sometimes start out the Christian life strong, with the best of intentions of living totally for the Lord. But then certain things happen that tempt them to stray from their commitment. Conflicts occur in the family, there may be clashes with the boss, illnesses may occur, finances may run short, the children may not behave as well as they should, other time pressures may crowd out devotions, and so on.

The wonderful thing about God's Word is that it goes directly to the heart of these issues. God designed us and provided the "user's manual," the Bible, for how we can live with the peace and joy He intended us to have, regardless of the circumstances. Do we still sin? Yes. We already know this by considering how many times we fail to love God's way. Is it always easy to live God's way in spite of our feelings? No. But the Bible and the Holy Spirit provide the resources we need to have hope and victory in these difficult situations. We need to recognize that tests and temptations are a regular part of life and then apply God's practical principles in the power of the Holy Spirit to have victory.

A. The Christian's walk

   1. Let's start by finding out what God says about our walk (some versions use "live" instead of "walk") as a Christian. There are many passages in the New Testament about the believer's walk in Christ. Read *Ephesians 2:1-10.* What do *verses 2* and *10* say about our walk?

      2. Verse 2: _____

      3. Verse 10: _____

      Before we came to Christ, we walked according to the ways of this world. But God made us alive together with Christ *(verse 5).* He transformed us, enabling us to walk by faith *(Galatians 2:20),* and even prepared the good works for us to "walk in" *(Ephesians 2:10).*

© BIBLICAL COUNSELING FOUNDATION

LESSON 2

WHAT DOES THE BIBLE SAY ABOUT
TESTS, TEMPTATIONS, AND PROBLEMS?

What does *Ephesians 2:4* say that our motivation for good works should be?

4. _____

Our motivation for good works is His great love and mercy toward us. Our works are in response to God's love, not an attempt to pay Him back. We can never pay God back for the priceless gift of salvation. We serve the Lord out of deep gratitude. Perhaps an illustration might be helpful.

ILLUSTRATION: A woman had a very unloving husband. Every day before he went to work, he would make a long list of tasks she was to complete before he returned home. No matter how hard she tried to complete the tasks, she never was successful. So, every night he would scold her for what he considered a very poor performance. Her life with this husband was very hard.

After a time, the husband died and a few years later she married another man who was kind and loving. They had a wonderful relationship and she was very happy.

One day as she was cleaning their home, she came across one of the lists of tasks that her former husband had written for her to do. As she looked at the list, she was amazed to discover that while she could not complete the list for the former husband no matter how hard she tried, she was now accomplishing *all* those things for her new husband.

The key application of this illustration is that before salvation, it was impossible to keep the Lord's commands consistently. When you are saved, you have a loving relationship espoused (engaged) to the Lord. Following Him is not a matter of merely following a set of rules. Following His commands is not an exercise in legalistic dos and don'ts. It is not a way to earn our salvation or to gain favor with God to balance out our sin. It is a loving response to what God has so amazingly and marvelously done for us. It is now a matter of loving obedience in the empowering of the Holy Spirit.

---

2. What does *Galatians 5:16* say about our walk?

5. _____

God says that we are to walk by the Spirit so that we will not carry out the desire of the flesh. But even though we have been crucified with Christ, and have a new power to resist sin that we did not have before, our fleshly desires are still with us. What does God say in *Galatians 5:17* about our daily struggle with sin?

6. _____

_____

The Spirit and the flesh are set against one another, and it does not take very long for our flesh to show itself. We are tempted to respond to our own spouse with impatience, to be angry with our children, to argue with the boss, and to be fearful about financial matters or an illness. We can exhibit, even as believers, behavior that is very similar to the deeds of the flesh referred to in *Galatians 5:19-20.* There are many ways that our old manner

© BIBLICAL COUNSELING FOUNDATION

LESSON 2

WHAT DOES THE BIBLE SAY ABOUT
TESTS, TEMPTATIONS, AND PROBLEMS?

of life comes out, even though we are new creations in Christ. We still sin. Our worldly inclinations are still there.

3. Thankfully, God also shows how different we can be as believers, by being filled with (controlled by) the Spirit *(Ephesians 5:18)* and exhibiting the fruit of the Spirit. List the characteristics of the fruit here, from *Galatians 5:22-23*.

    7. _____

    _____

The extent to which we exhibit the fruit of the Spirit is an indicator of our walk with Christ. It demonstrates our love and gratitude in response to what God has done for us. As we develop a regular pattern of walking in the Spirit, of exhibiting the Spirit's fruit, we grow in maturity and are better equipped to help others. God allows trials in our life as part of the maturing process, as we will see in the next section.

B. The daily challenge of tests and temptations

Every believer will encounter trials in life. Satan seeks to defeat you by tempting you to trust your own wisdom, to live according to your self-centered feelings, and to gratify the desires of your flesh. In contrast, God's will is for you to be an overwhelming conqueror in all of these trials for His honor and glory.

Your daily walk with Christ is filled with opportunities either to walk by your fleshly desires or to walk by the Spirit. Just as Jesus prepared His disciples for this battle, God wants to prepare you (to equip you) to have victory. So let's see what God says about the nature of trials, tests, and temptations.

1. Read *I Peter 1:6-7*. What is more precious than gold?

    8. _____

    _____

    a. The word in this passage for "test" or "refine" means to be proved, such as metals are tried by fire and thus are purified. The word "prove" does not mean to show to be true or false as in "prove it to me," but it is used in the good sense and means to "show forth." The emphasis in this passage is to prove someone good and acceptable.

    b. Read *I Peter 4:12-13*. What does God say about trials in this passage?

    9. _____

    _____

    c. Can you think of any trials that you have been "surprised" by in your life?

    10. _____

    What does this passage tell you about that trial?

    11. _____

© BIBLICAL COUNSELING FOUNDATION

LESSON 2

WHAT DOES THE BIBLE SAY ABOUT
TESTS, TEMPTATIONS, AND PROBLEMS?

You should not be surprised when trials come, even when they are intense and seem fiery. Consider the following illustration:

> **ILLUSTRATION:** Years ago when Amy Carmichael was ministering in India as a missionary, she went to a goldsmith to find out how gold was purified so that she could understand how God "tests" or "proves" us. The goldsmith placed in the pot old jewelry, gold bars, and ore, which all seemed to have varying degrees of purity. She watched as the gold was being melted in a pot placed over an intense fire. As the material in the pot heated, smoke began to rise from the pot. The goldsmith explained that if she would look down into the pot, Amy would notice scum floating on the surface. The scum, he explained, is called "dross" and must be burned off. At one point, Amy asked the goldsmith how he would know that the gold was purified. He answered that the gold would be pure when he could look down into it and see a perfect reflection of his face.
>
> In the same way, God tests or proves believers so that they may reflect the image of Christ in their lives.
>
> Looking beyond Amy Carmichael's writings, remember that the goldsmith is not finished with the gold, even when it has been purified. He then molds, forms, pounds, and etches the gold to make it into something useful and beautiful. God does not necessarily remove us from a circumstance, but while we are being purified, He continues His work in our lives to make us useful vessels for His service.

We are going to study more about tests and temptations, but right now, you may want to pause and give Him thanks for the difficulty you are now facing and how He is using it in your life.

2. Read *James 1:13-14.* Who is *not* the source of temptation?

   12. _____

   In this passage, what *is* a source of temptation?

   13. _____

   A temptation, which does not originate from God, is an enticement for you to disobey God's Word and to gratify your fleshly desires. When you yield to temptation, you inevitably experience consequences.

   a. It is important to note that temptations, in and of themselves, are not sins. We know this because we read in *Hebrews 4:15* that Jesus was tempted, but did not sin.

   b. Read *I John 2:16.* What are the three areas of temptation listed here?

      14. _____

      _____

      _____

© BIBLICAL COUNSELING FOUNDATION

LESSON 2

WHAT DOES THE BIBLE SAY ABOUT
TESTS, TEMPTATIONS, AND PROBLEMS?

    c. There are many types of temptations. Can you give an example in each of the above categories?

       15. _____

       _____

       _____

    Every difficult circumstance that comes into your life can be seen as a test from God or as a temptation to sin (either through your own flesh, the world, or through Satan). So in every difficulty, your choice is either to stand firm and grow in Christlikeness or to sin and suffer the consequences. To respond biblically to the circumstance, you do not need to focus on trying to determine if it is a test or a temptation. Rather, in every difficulty you have an opportunity to practice Christlikeness by obeying God's Word, thus giving honor to Jesus Christ.

C. What was the most significant truth you learned in completing this lesson?

    16. _____

    _____

17

D. For the next lesson:

    1. Before starting the next lesson, be sure to recite *I Peter 4:12* to someone.

    2. Study Lesson 3 and answer the questions. Do a little bit of the lesson each day.

    3. Check your answers in the back of the booklet.

    In Lesson 3, we will look at an example of a problem that develops in the life of a student and see that problem from a scriptural viewpoint. We'll also learn more in Lesson 4 about the hope we have in seeing and responding to tests and temptations God's way.

© BIBLICAL COUNSELING FOUNDATION

18

© BIBLICAL COUNSELING FOUNDATION

LESSON 3

THE DOWNWARD SPIRAL OF DEFEAT

Before you begin this lesson, ask for God's help in understanding His Word and for wisdom and strength to apply what you learn in the power of the Holy Spirit.

Begin memorizing *I Corinthians 10:13* and prepare to recite this passage before the next lesson.

A. The downward spiral

When a believer strays away from fellowship with the Lord, it is usually not a sharp drop of rebellion, but a spiritual slice away from God's way over a period of time. The Bible indicates that a person's life will become progressively more set in sin with correspondingly graver consequences if he continues to live according to man's way. A biblical illustration of this downward spiral is found in *Romans 1:18-32*.

Read *verses 18-20* and note that man's separation from God is not a matter of a lack of knowledge. So what is the issue?

1. _____

In *verse 19,* we see that God reveals Himself to mankind from within man by means of man's conscience, and in *verse 20,* God reveals Himself from outside man by means of God's creation. The issue is not how much you know about God — it is how you respond to what you know of Him that shows your focus. The fact is that man willfully rejects God.

Read *verses 21-23.* What are the consequences in people's lives when they reject God?

2. _____

_____

It seems incredible that people will worship animals and even images they have carved out of wood. Yet, this shows how foolish man can be when his primary objective is to create an idol that he can manipulate to achieve his own foolish desires. As long as man creates the idols he chooses to worship, he maintains control.

Note in *verses 24, 26,* and *28* that *"God gave them over"* to their own lusts and depravity. Why? Because often, the only thing that will get a fool's attention is consequences. God helps them see the consequences of their actions so that they may see their error and may be encouraged to repent.

It is interesting to note that in *verses 26-27,* homosexuality is presented as an example of the continuing slide into sin.

Read *verse 32.* How did they sink to the lowest depth?

3. _____

Let's look at the development of a problem by taking the example of a student.

© BIBLICAL COUNSELING FOUNDATION

LESSON 3

THE DOWNWARD SPIRAL OF DEFEAT

> **ILLUSTRATION:** Let's assume that a Christian student just arrived at his room at school and that this is the first time he is living away from home. His parents have provided funds for his schooling and they have exhorted him to study diligently.
>
> During his first day of classes, each teacher also exhorted him to study diligently every evening. But when it was time to study, his roommates asked him to go with them to the student recreation center on campus. He remembered his responsibility to study; but because he was focused on self at the heart level, he soon decided to delay studying and, instead, went to the center with his roommates. He was starting down the spiral as the focus of his sinful heart was being manifested by sinful deeds. He enjoyed himself so much that when he returned to his room, it was too late to study.
>
> The next day, he was anxious in class, but none of his teachers called on him for an answer. He was extremely relieved!
>
> In the evening, it was a little easier to ignore his studies and, once again, to go to the recreation center with his companions.
>
> As a result of not studying, the student began to worry about failing the course. When his parents wrote and asked about his studies, he lied to them and told them he was doing fine. As you can see, he was sliding further down the spiral.
>
> Finally, in desperation, he cheated on his exams and failed anyway. As a result, he felt guilty and depressed.

Now in order to understand the succession of this process, we need to see what is happening at three different levels. What are the names of the three levels typed in **boldface** print on the chart on the next page?

4. _____

_____

_____

You can see the examples of the student's continuation down the spiral, from the initial temptation to the increasing progression of sin. The student's focus on self (heart level) led to the unbiblical deeds (the doing level). Each sin made it easier to commit another sin. As he continued to sin, he became depressed (the feeling level). You might have even seen this progression at some point in your own life or in the life of a friend or family member.

LESSON 3

THE DOWNWARD SPIRAL OF DEFEAT

THE DOWNWARD SPIRAL

1. **Heart level**

    Focus on self *(Luke 9:23-24)*

2. **Doing level (unbiblical deeds)**

    Tempted to follow fleshly desires instead of a commitment to God (**thought life**) *(Galatians 5:16-17; Ephesians 2:3; Titus 2:11-12)*

    Doesn't study (**actions**) *(II Thessalonians 3:11)*

    Keeps bad company (**actions**) *(Proverbs 1:10-19, 24:1; I Corinthians 15:33)*

    Worries about failing course (**thought life**) *(Proverbs 12:25a; Philippians 4:6)*

    Lies to parents about readiness for exams (**words**) *(Ephesians 4:25; Colossians 3:9)*

    Cheats on exams (**actions**) *(Exodus 20:15; Ephesians 4:28)*

    Fails course (consequence) *(Proverbs 28:13; Colossians 3:25)*

3. **Feeling level**

    Depression, despair, guilt feelings *(Psalm 38:4-8)*

B. Understanding the three levels of the problem

1. **Heart level** — The world's focus regarding the heart is primarily on the emotions. But what do the Scriptures say about the heart?

    a. The "heart" refers to one's character or inner life with its desires and purpose for living (see the following Scriptures as examples: *Jeremiah 32:38-41; Ezekiel 11:21; Mark 3:5; Luke 9:47; Acts 2:46-47, 4:32; Romans 2:5*).

    b. Read *Jeremiah 17:9-10*. Who is the only one who is able to see a person's heart completely?

        5. _____

        Notice that in *verse 10*, even though God knows our hearts fully, He deals with us at the "deeds" or doing level.

    c. Read *Luke 5:22*. In this passage, to what does Jesus liken the heart?

        6. _____

        We see here that Jesus mentioned reasoning as being in the heart. Notice that Jesus associates the heart with the mind, not with feelings or emotions.

© BIBLICAL COUNSELING FOUNDATION

LESSON 3

THE DOWNWARD SPIRAL OF DEFEAT

2. **Doing Level** — Deeds, not feelings, are the primary *observable* indicators of the inner person. Read *Matthew 15:18-19.* List all the sinful deeds you see in these verses, grouped by whether they are thoughts, speech, or actions.

7. Thoughts: _____

8. Speech: _____

9. Actions: _____

a. In the Scriptures, there is a significant emphasis on keeping God's commandments. You may wonder why there are so many more Scripture verses on doing the Word than there are on explaining a believer's position in Christ. Which do you think is more difficult: understanding your position in Christ or consistently doing the Word?

10. _____

b. Scripture emphasizes doing the Word not because it is more important than understanding your position in Christ, but because doing the Word consistently is harder! The Lord in His grace typically gives us the most instruction in the very areas where it is the hardest to follow Him, or where we tend to go our own direction.

3. **Feeling level**

a. How a person feels is not a reliable indication of the condition of a person's heart. For example, King David experienced many horrible feelings (both in his emotions and in his body) while he tried to hide his sin with Bathsheba. In this case, the feelings accurately indicated the problem of his heart when he tried to hide his adultery with Bathsheba for about a year. On the other hand, the Israelites rejoiced as they sinned while they became drunk, worshiped the golden calf, and committed sensuality and immorality. Even though they temporarily felt good, the feelings were not accurate indicators of the wickedness in their hearts. Can you think of situations in which a person may not have good feelings, and yet there is no sin involved?

11. _____

_____

Unpleasant feelings could be the result of an illness, such as the flu. A chemical or hormonal imbalance could cause feelings of gloom even though there may be nothing wrong at the heart level.

Feelings are involuntary. They are caused indirectly, not directly. Feelings are not willed into being. They are indicators, not instigators. Feelings, in and of themselves, are not sin.

How do we know that feelings are not sin and that God does not hold us responsible for changing our feelings?

12. _____

© BIBLICAL COUNSELING FOUNDATION

LESSON 3

THE DOWNWARD SPIRAL OF DEFEAT

We are never commanded anywhere in the Scriptures to change our feelings. God only commands us to change from our sinful deeds. Being patient does not feel good, but we are commanded to be patient regardless of our feelings.

b. Because most feelings are involuntary responses to a person's thoughts, speech, or actions that arise in the context of the circumstances of life, feelings may provide clues that a person is sinning. Therefore, feelings should not be ignored. Consider the following illustration.

ILLUSTRATION: A good way to understand feelings is to compare them to the oil warning light in a car. The purpose of the warning light is to communicate that there is something wrong under the hood. When one is driving along on the highway and the oil light comes on, what types of things may be wrong?

13. _____

_____

Sometimes, the oil light itself may be malfunctioning. For all of these situations, even the one with the malfunctioning oil light, the light is a signal that the driver needs to examine the automobile and determine what the real problem is. Then, as necessary, he must take corrective action as a result of this examination. If the driver ignores or punches out the warning light because it is a nuisance, he may soon find himself sitting behind the wheel of a vehicle that has a serious problem.

In the same way, if you ignore or merely soothe your feelings and do not correct the underlying problem, you may have more serious problems later. You may actually be putting a bandage on a guilty conscience that is being pricked by the Holy Spirit.

---

c. God gave us feelings for our good. Feelings usually provide the first indication that we need to pay attention to what is happening, either good or bad. Keep in mind, however, that while feelings are helpful indicators, we are not to follow our feelings. God tells us to obey whether we feel like it or not, and He enables us to obey.

Now let's get back to the student we described earlier. Suppose he were to come to you for help when he was at the bottom of his downward spiral. Remember, you would not know immediately what led to his depression. What problem do you think he would present to you (put a check beside your answer below):

- ☐ a. His feelings of being depressed;
- ☐ b. The fact that he lied and cheated (the doing level); or
- ☐ c. The fact that he is a sinful, self-centered person (the heart level)?

Most people in that situation would present to you their feelings of being depressed. The student may want to get rid of the feelings associated with depression.

© BIBLICAL COUNSELING FOUNDATION

LESSON 3

THE DOWNWARD SPIRAL OF DEFEAT

Some might say that his depression is caused by traumatic events that may have happened in the distant past and, therefore, a thorough analysis, often reaching back to early childhood, must be conducted. This analysis often takes months and even years.

Others would say he should concentrate on fixing his feelings about himself. They would encourage him to love himself more because they believe his depression is caused by low self-esteem.

Some would merely prescribe particular pills ignoring the possibility that the same feelings may be caused by sinful behavior.

Where was the student's focus of attention as he went through the downward spiral? On himself or on his concern for others?

14. _____

If he had considered love for God and others, he would have regarded his parents' counsel and their investment in him more highly by being responsible and diligent in his studies. He would have been more concerned about his fellow students' studies. He would have respected the efforts of his teachers. The student was focused on himself and not on the interests of others. Contrary to the world's philosophies, the Bible assures the student that he can have victory quickly and completely by confessing his sin and placing himself under the control of the Holy Spirit. Not only that, but he can be used by God in the lives of others.

C. What was the most significant truth you learned in completing this lesson?

15. _____

_____

D. For the next lesson:

1. Before starting the next lesson, be sure to recite *I Corinthians 10:13* to someone.

2. Study Lesson 4 and answer the questions. Do a little bit of the lesson each day.

3. Check your answers in the back of the booklet.

In Lesson 4, we will see the hope that is available to us in the midst of our trials. In Lesson 5 we will determine from the Word of God what steps we must take to get out of the downward spiral and travel the upward path to victory.

LESSON 4

BIBLICAL HOPE

Before you begin this lesson, ask for God's help in understanding His Word and for wisdom and strength to apply what you learn in the power of the Holy Spirit.

Begin memorizing *Romans 8:28-29* and prepare to recite this passage before the next lesson.

The hope that God has provided for you is not merely a wish. Your hope is not dependent on other people, possessions, or circumstances. Instead, biblical hope is an application of your faith that supplies a confident expectation in God's fulfillment of His promises. Coupled with faith and love, hope is part of the abiding characteristics in a believer's life *(based on Psalm 39:7; Lamentations 3:21-24; Romans 5:1-5; I Corinthians 13:13; I Thessalonians 1:2-3; Hebrews 6:19; I Peter 1:3)*.

Let's look at some biblical principles on the subject of hope.

A. Biblical principles on the subject of hope.

   1. *Principle of hope 1* — Those in Christ are freed from the power and penalty of sin *(Romans 6:6-7, 14, 18, 23; I John 1:9)*.

      a. Read *Romans 6:6-7*.

         Let's say that a person has a life-dominating practice of sin, such as drunkenness. The Bible calls drunkenness sin, so how can it possibly bring hope to point out that the one who is drunk is committing sin and is not doomed by an illness?

         1. _____

         _____

         Sin can be confessed immediately, and fellowship with God can be restored. Relieving the symptoms of drunkenness, anger, fear, lust, drug abuse, immorality, etc. without dealing with sin is shallow and would, at most, only provide artificial and temporary comfort. This does not deal with the basic problem of sin, and thus does not provide biblical hope.

         No sinner is beyond the reach of God even though he may have placed himself under the control of sin for many years. After becoming a believer, he can stop his drinking immediately and live victoriously by God's power. Yes, he may still have strong cravings for a long time (and perhaps for his whole life), but he does not ever have to yield to temptation again. This brings tremendous hope to someone who has been a drunkard for years and has tried many times to break his bondage to alcohol. He is finally free and empowered by God to live in great victory.

      b. Read *Romans 6:18*. What does God say about believers?

         2. _____

         In *verse 7* we read that you are set free from sin, but in *verse 18* you are a slave to righteousness. You go from being a slave to sin to being a slave to righteousness. Does that sound like freedom to you? Many would say it does not.

25

© BIBLICAL COUNSELING FOUNDATION

LESSON 4

BIBLICAL HOPE

> ***ILLUSTRATION:*** Think about a guitar or violin string. Sometimes a string breaks and it must be replaced. When you purchase a new string it usually comes in a package coiled up all by itself. When you take it out of the package it looks free, but really it is only loose. It is not truly free until it is put on the instrument and the proper tension is applied for it to sound on pitch. Only then is it finally free to fulfill its purpose and be played by the musician. In the same way, it is only when you are attached to the Lord (i.e., only when you are saved), that you are truly free. Only then are you able to live in the tensions of life, to respond in God's way, and to fulfill the purpose for which He created you.

Keep in mind that dealing with sin in a person's life is of first importance, because sin affects his fellowship with God. When sin is confessed and repentance takes place, the deeper problem of the heart is dealt with, and there is immediate biblical hope. This does not mean that the person will be totally removed from the temptation. For example, someone who has been a drunkard for many years might still face cravings in his body, but for the first time, when he becomes a child of God, he no longer has to yield to sin.

2. *Principle of hope 2* — God will not allow believers to be tested or tempted beyond what they can bear. He gives you His grace and strength to endure every test and resist every temptation so that you never have to sin *(I Corinthians 10:13; Philippians 4:13; Hebrews 4:15-16; II Peter 2:4-9)*.

   Read *I Corinthians 10:13*. What does God say about temptation in this verse?

   3. _____

   _____

   _____

   _____

God says that there is *no* temptation that He has not also given you the strength and resources to overcome. In other words, God never allows you to be in a position where you *must* sin. This is great hope.

© BIBLICAL COUNSELING FOUNDATION

LESSON 4

BIBLICAL HOPE

> ***ILLUSTRATION:*** Because of greed, many merchants for hundreds of years up to the late 19th century would send ships out as empty as possible to collect cargo and treasure. On the return trip, they would direct the captains to overload the ships. On the first leg of the journey, ships would be so light (with no load) that they would be tossed to and fro in storms and would be prone to capsize. On the return, the ships would be so full that they would sometimes sink in turbulent seas, riding too low in the water. As a result, Samuel Plimsoll, a member of the British Parliament, initiated a bill to require all ships to have a horizontal line painted on their hulls to show the ideal weight with which they should be loaded for safety. The bill became law, and even today, this line is still painted on ships. This "ideal weight" line is known as the "Plimsoll line."
>
> In the same way, God places His own "ideal weight" line on every believer. Although a believer can be heavily burdened, God knows how much weight (trials) each one needs and can face; and no believer ever needs to be overcome by any "weight" of life that will cause him to sink spiritually. God will never allow anything into a believer's life that will cause him to fall to temptation and sin.
>
> While *I Corinthians 10:13* provides great hope, it presents a warning at the same time. If a person gives in to a temptation, he cannot blame anything or anyone else for his sin.

It is also important to note that in *I Corinthians 10:13,* God states there is an escape. From what is the escape?

4. _____

_____

Note that the situation may not go away. It may even intensify. But God says that you will be able not only to face and deal with any difficulty of life, but also to endure it. Enduring the difficulty means to live in victory whether or not the difficulty disappears. This is a marvelous hope. But it is also sobering, because when you sin, it is not because circumstances are too much for you to bear. Instead, you sin because you choose to do so. Sin involves a choice.

3. *Principle of hope 3* — A godly response to tests and temptations will develop and mature you in Christ *(James 1:2-4).* He never devises evil or harm for you; rather His plans for you are for good *(Genesis 50:20; Jeremiah 29:11-13; Romans 8:28-29).*

   a. Read *James 1:2-4.* What does God say in this passage about your trials?

   5. _____

   _____

   God tells us that every trial is an *opportunity* to become more mature. Trials are not obstacles to spiritual growth when you respond to them in a biblical manner. Remember the "Plimsoll line"? God allows just enough trials to encourage maximum growth, neither too few trials nor too many.

© BIBLICAL COUNSELING FOUNDATION

LESSON 4

BIBLICAL HOPE

The phrase "counting (or considering) it all joy" in this passage is not dependent on feelings. It indicates an inner contentment and satisfaction that comes from God, independent of circumstances. A good example is found in *Hebrews 12:2.* What was the joy set before Jesus?

6. _____

b. Read *Matthew 26:39.* Did Jesus enjoy going to the cross?

7. _____

As Jesus was going through His most difficult trial (the crucifixion and separation from His Father), His focus was on the end result — that after He completed His mission, He would be back with His Father.

You can consider it all joy when you go through a trial, knowing that you will come out of it more mature, even though you do not "enjoy" going through it. "Joy" and "enjoy" are two different things.

ILLUSTRATION: Certain medicines include ingredients that, if taken separately or included in the medicine in the wrong amount, could kill a person. However, because these ingredients are mixed in the right amount, they are very beneficial. For example, if taken in the right amount nitroglycerin can be a lifesaver when a person is having a heart attack. It is also a powerful explosive that can destroy many lives.

In the same way, God actively works out His plan and always does what is good for us even if He must discipline us in the process. We may view certain painful experiences as bad, but God always works them together for good to those who love Him and are called according to His purpose.

---

c. What is the "good" for you according to *Romans 8:29?*

8. _____

d. Read *Genesis 50:20.* What were some of the trials Joseph faced? Read the following passages and list the trials and injustices that God allowed in his life:

9. *Genesis 37:23-28* — _____

10. *Genesis 39:11-20* — _____

_____

11. *Genesis 40:12-14, 23* — _____

In all these, Joseph did not take revenge or complain. Rather, he trusted the Lord to use these events for good. He did not know exactly how they might be used in his life, but he knew that God was faithful.

4. *Principle of hope 4* — No one is doomed to spiritual defeat because of another human being's sin *(Ezekiel 18:1-20).* God sovereignly protects His children and insures that no believer can be separated from His love *(Romans 8:38-39).* No one can prevent a person

---

© BIBLICAL COUNSELING FOUNDATION

LESSON 4

BIBLICAL HOPE

from receiving God's protection, and no one can prevent God from providing a person with the power to have victory in his or her life.

a. Read *Ezekiel 18:1-20.* This passage concerns a false proverb that had arisen among the children of Israel. What was the erroneous proverb (see *verse 2)?*

12. _____

What is God's response in *verses 3* and *4?*

13. _____

_____

Note that children are not doomed to follow their parents' sinful life styles. This is tremendous hope. Have you ever heard someone say "His parents were like this, so is it any wonder that he s like this himself?" This is similar to the proverb that the Israelites were using in *verse 2.* Sometimes parents are blamed for their children's sinful behavior. Are parents responsible before God to be good parents? Of course they are! But even if they are not godly parents, the believing children can be godly.

To emphasize this point, God describes a righteous man in *verses 5-9* who has a violent son, as we see described in *verses 10-13.* Then we see in *verses 14-17* that this violent son, in turn, has a son who has observed all the evil acts that his father has done and yet rejects his father's behavior and lives a very righteous life. Notice that this son was present and saw all that his very wicked father did, yet he did not sin. Neither was he scarred for life. *Verse 20* indicates that we need not have false guilt for someone else's sin. It is important that parents do not live in defeat when their children go astray as adults.

b. Now, what about the Scripture passage that says the sins of the father will be visited on the children to the third and fourth generation? (See, for example, *Deuteronomy 5:9.*) God's Law clearly placed the blame for an individual's sins on that individual alone *(Deuteronomy 24:16).* However, the *physical* consequences of an individual's sins are often experienced by others closely related to the offender. This is what is being discussed in *Deuteronomy 5:9.* What are some examples of sin reaping physical consequences to others not responsible for the sin?

14. _____

_____

_____

You may be wondering why God allows sinners to harm innocent people physically. If someone were to aim a pistol directly at you and pull the trigger, God would not necessarily stop the bullet in midair just because you are innocent. God allows us to make choices either to obey or disobey Him. If He did not allow us to choose, we would merely be robots and incapable of love since love is a choice.

© BIBLICAL COUNSELING FOUNDATION

LESSON 4

BIBLICAL HOPE

But the wonderful truth is that while God may allow us to experience *physical* consequences of someone else's sins, He will never allow anything or anyone to affect our *spiritual* condition, and our spiritual condition is far more important than our physical condition. God sovereignly protects us from spiritual harm. And just because we may be tempted or weak in a particular area of our life does not mean that we *must* commit that sin. By God's grace we can say "no" to ungodliness and live in victory over sin.

5. *Principle of hope 5* — When you confess your sins, God forgives and cleanses you.

   Read *I John 1:9.* What hope about problems is offered in this verse?

   15. _____

   _____

   Isn't it wonderful to know that even when a person fails miserably, he can start afresh?

B. What was the most significant truth you learned in completing this lesson?

   16. _____

   _____

C. For the next lesson:

   1. Before starting the next lesson, be sure to recite *Romans 8:28-29* to someone.

   2. Study Lesson 5 and answer the questions. Do a little bit of the lesson each day.

   3. Check your answers in the back of the booklet.

   In Lesson 4 we have seen that God has given us great hope and powerful resources for change. In Lesson 5 we will see that He has also designed a *process* for change.

© BIBLICAL COUNSELING FOUNDATION

LESSON 5

BIBLICAL CHANGE:
DEALING WITH PROBLEMS GOD'S WAY

Before you begin this lesson, ask for God's help in understanding His Word and for wisdom and strength to apply what you learn in the power of the Holy Spirit.

Begin memorizing *Ephesians 4:22, 24* and prepare to recite this passage before the next lesson.

You saw earlier that the Christian life is about walking in God's way. You are in the process of being conformed to the image of Christ *(Romans 8:29)*, walking not according to the flesh but according to the Spirit. Change is not easy at times, and it is a life-long process, because it involves the ongoing battle between the flesh and the Spirit. You make many choices each day: whether you are going to go God's way, or fulfill your own desires.

A. Evaluate what you need to change in your life.

1. As you have learned, God holds you responsible for faithfulness to keep His commandments, i.e., doing His Word. He does not hold you responsible for results. The place to begin the process of biblical change is within the present trial, temptation, or problem in your life. God says that He will give us answers. But many people will say, "I asked God for wisdom, but I didn't receive it." Why? Because they asked the wrong questions or had a wrong motivation.

   Read *James 1:2-5*. For what situation does God promise wisdom?

   1. _____

   Notice the context of this passage. The first verses in this passage are about trials. The Lord will give us wisdom, but there are conditions. First, it is for the current trial that you are to seek wisdom. *Verses 2-4* should not be disconnected from *verse 5*. Second, God says in *verse 6* that you are to ask in faith without doubting. Also read *verse 22*. What does God say to you if you do not obey?

   2. _____

   It is important to remember that you keep God's commandments in the present, not in the past or the future. Read *Hebrews 4:16*. At what time does God give you His grace?

   3. _____

   Your faith is tested in the present trial. Answers to problems are not difficult to find if you focus on your present responsibilities, and do not worry about the future.

2. Your evaluation must be based on God's standard for you. Read *Matthew 22:37-40*. What are the two commandments Jesus states in this passage?

   4. _____

   Note that all of the commands listed in the Scriptures (the Law and the Prophets) depend on these two laws. Isn't that amazing? The Lord has made this very simple for the Christian to understand. In any situation, all we need to ask ourselves is, "What is the loving thing to do?" The Christian life is not complicated. Even a small child can practice loving God and others. Yet, we often stumble and wonder what we should do. So why do we stumble over this? Let's look more closely at what God says the focus of your life should be.

31

© BIBLICAL COUNSELING FOUNDATION

LESSON 5

BIBLICAL CHANGE:
DEALING WITH PROBLEMS GOD'S WAY

3. Biblical love is an act of the will in obedience to God and is not dependent on feelings. One of the best known passages from the Bible on this subject is *I Corinthians 13,* "the love chapter." Read *verses 4-8* of *I Corinthians 13.* Each of these characteristics of love illustrates the giving up of selfish desires and putting God and others first.

4. Love is particularly tested when you do not *feel* like being loving. For example, it is easy to be patient when things are going well: lines at the grocery store are short, you don't get stuck in traffic, or the children are being well-behaved. But you really find out how patient you are when the lines are long, traffic is stop-and-go, and the children are not cooperating. These circumstances give you an opportunity to practice patience.

   Let's take a few of the statements in *I Corinthians 13:4-8* and put them in the context of situations where it is hard to love.

   - Love is kind, even when others may be unkind to you.

   - Love is not jealous, even when others are being noticed or rewarded more than you.

   - Love does not brag, even when you want others to take more notice of your accomplishments.

   - Love does not seek its own; rather, as an act of the will, it seeks to serve and not be served.

   - Love is not provoked, even when others attempt to provoke you or you are tempted to strike out at something or someone.

   - Love does not even take into account a wrong suffered.

   Responding in love under these circumstances is not easy, but it is the standard to which God calls believers. Believers especially have an opportunity for demonstrating the difference Christ makes in their lives when they respond in love even when going through a difficult circumstance. And there are many opportunities to practice biblical love each day, both with other believers as well as with those outside the faith. List at least two areas of love mentioned in *I Corinthians 13:4-8* that you have difficulty demonstrating.

   5. _____

   _____

   A good way to start your evaluation is to list the specific ways in which you are not loving in the areas that you just listed.

B. Taking the log out of your eye

   Be careful that if your problem area involves someone else, you do not focus on trying to get the other person to change. One temptation is to blame a circumstance or someone else for your problems. God says that the way to deal with a problem is not to blame others or the circumstances, but first to examine self.

© BIBLICAL COUNSELING FOUNDATION

LESSON 5

BIBLICAL CHANGE:
DEALING WITH PROBLEMS GOD'S WAY

Read *Matthew 7:1-5.* In *verse 1,* the word "judge" means to pass sentence on someone, as in a courtroom. Jesus said that you are *not* to do this, but in *verse 5,* what are you to do first, before dealing with anyone else's failures?

6. _____

Only when you take the log out of your own eyes will you see clearly to take the speck out of your brothers' eyes. Think of it this way. When a speck of dust gets into your eye, what happens? Even with the tiny speck, your eye begins to water and you cannot see clearly. Your vision becomes distorted and things may even seem to be magnified or abnormal. So imagine what it would be like if you had a log in your eye! It is obvious that you would need to remove the log before you could see clearly to help someone else.

In some ways, this is a very dangerous Bible Study. If you listen to the teaching from the Scriptures but do not apply it in your own life (i.e., you do not take the log out of your own eye), what does Jesus say about you?

7. _____

This is important because, according to *verse 5,* you are responsible to do more than simply point out the speck in the eyes of others. What is that responsibility?

8. _____

You have an additional responsibility to get involved in their lives and serve them as you help them remove the speck from their eyes. You will see this responsibility explained more fully in Lesson 6.

So how do you take the log out of your own eye? God has provided a specific biblical process for change.

C. The biblical process for change.

1. To understand that biblical change is a process, let's start by reading *Ephesians 4:22-24.* Notice that at the beginning of *verse 22* you are told to deal with the *manner* of life of the old self. This passage describes the biblical principle of putting off the old way of living and putting on the righteous practices of the new self. While the new self has been put on at salvation, the old way of living must be decisively put off (that is, laid aside completely and permanently). The words "lay aside" or "put off" are not telling us to remove temporarily, but the command is to ' put away" sinful practices from our lives. At the same time, the righteous *practices* of the new self must be put on. *Verses 25* through *32* provide practical examples of how the principle works. This is a process that continues in the believer's life until death. Lasting change doesn't take place merely by putting off — both "put-ons" and "put-offs" must be practiced simultaneously.

    As you study the Word, you will discover many "put-offs" and "put-ons" in the Scripture passages. One way of keeping track of the "put-offs" and "put-ons" is to write a minus (-) symbol above each Scripture portion that lists a "put-off" and a plus (+) symbol above each portion that lists a "put-on."

33

© BIBLICAL COUNSELING FOUNDATION

LESSON 5

BIBLICAL CHANGE:
DEALING WITH PROBLEMS GOD'S WAY

2. List below the various "put-offs" and "put-ons" you see in *Ephesians 4:25-32.* As you read each verse, place a minus (-) symbol above each "put-off" and a plus (+) symbol above each "put-on."

   a. *Verse 25*

      9. "Put-off": _____

      10. "Put-on": _____

      Is it possible for someone to put off lying and never put on speaking the truth? If so, how?

      11. _____

      Note that merely putting off falsehood does not necessarily mean that lasting change has taken place. Rather than yielding to the temptation to lie to someone, you are to speak the truth to that very individual. Both the "put-off" and the "put-ons" must be practiced at the same time.

   b. *Verse 28*

      12. "Put-off": _____

      13. "Put-on": _____

      If a robber has stopped robbing after stealing a million dollars, does that mean that he is no longer a robber?

      14. _____

      Note that to change completely, he must earn money by working for it and then share with those in need. Then, he has become a giver rather than a taker.

   c. *Verse 29*

      15. "Put-off": _____

      16. "Put-on": _____

      _____

      Note that this is very different from saying, "If you cannot say anything nice, don't say anything at all."

   d. *Verses 31-32*

      17. "Put-off": _____

      18. "Put-on": _____

   Notice the pattern in these verses; for each "put-off" in the Bible, there is usually a "put-on," and often it is in the same passage. This correspondence of "put-offs" and "put-ons" is present throughout the Bible. God does not just tell you what to refrain from doing; He tells you what to do instead. ***WARNING:*** *You must be careful not to try to match "put-offs" and "put-ons" from unrelated passages or make your own selection of a "put-on"*

LESSON 5

BIBLICAL CHANGE:
DEALING WITH PROBLEMS GOD'S WAY

for a particular "put-off" listed in the Scriptures. If you replace God's instruction with what seems good to you, you will have difficulties.

D. Application to the student described in Lesson 3

Now let's get back to the student. Suppose he came to you and presented the problem to you only at the "feeling level." How would you help him at that point?

1. The first and most important thing that you would do to help the student in the illustration is to examine whether or not he is saved. Why should you deal with salvation first?

   19. _____

   _____

   _____

2. If he is not saved, he will not have the resources to apply God's solutions in a lasting, meaningful way. If you present God's solutions without dealing with his salvation, he may apply biblical principles temporarily in his own strength, but you will not have dealt with his most significant problem. You must be careful not to help him be satisfied without the Lord.

3. If he is a believer, he needs to examine in what ways he is failing to love God and others. It would not be difficult for him to remember that he disobeyed God by not studying diligently, by lying to his parents, by cheating on the exam, etc. If he repents of these sins and obeys God, the Lord will provide not only the power to change quickly and completely, but also the contentment that only He can give. The student can take the log out of his own eye, take the focus off himself, and begin demonstrating love for others. You will see how to take this further in Lesson 6.

E. What was the most significant truth you learned in completing this lesson?

   20. _____

   _____

F. For the next lesson:

1. Before starting the next lesson, be sure to recite *Ephesians 4:22, 24* to someone.

2. Study Lesson 6 and answer the questions. Do a little bit of the lesson each day.

3. Check your answers in the back of the booklet.

In the next lesson we will see the importance of being a doer of the Word.

35

© BIBLICAL COUNSELING FOUNDATION

36

© BIBLICAL COUNSELING FOUNDATION

LESSON 6

BIBLICAL PRACTICE:
YOUR DAILY WALK WITH CHRIST

Before you begin this lesson, ask for God's help in understanding His Word and for wisdom and strength to apply what you learn in the power of the Holy Spirit.

Begin memorizing *Luke 9:23-24* and prepare to recite this passage at the end of the Lesson 6.

Biblical practice is the element that makes the difference between being just a "hearer of the Word" and being a "doer of the Word." You can understand the problem, have hope, and know how to change, but if you do not *practice* the Word, you will be worse off. Read *Hebrews 5:12-14.* According to *verse 14,* what are the results when you do not practice God's Word?

1. _____

You will not stay at the same place in your spiritual life. What does God say in *James 1:22* will happen if you are not a doer of the Word?

2. _____

Notice that you delude *yourself.* No one else deludes you, or takes you unaware. You are not "robbed" of your peace and joy; you put yourself in that state.

From the beginning, God's instructions for living have been very simple. In the Garden of Eden, He gave Adam and Eve only one commandment. God's command was simple and He emphasized the importance of obedience. Jesus told the disciples the two greatest commandments — as we will see, they are very simple, but all encompassing. He also said that your focus must be to "lose" your life rather than to "save" your life. Let's study some principles about biblical practice.

A. Practice denying self and following Christ.

    1. Read *Luke 9:23-24.* In this passage, Jesus gives you His basic focus for living. You are to deny self, that is, take your focus off self. Notice that Jesus tells you to take up your cross daily. What is the cross a symbol of?

        3. _____

        Now, what is the "put-on" in this passage?

        4. _____

        What happens when you focus on saving (or finding) your life?

        5. _____

        In *verse 24,* we see how important this command is. If you concentrate on finding (or saving) your life, you will lose it. To understand the significance of this statement, let's consider how God created you to live.

        In the book of *Genesis,* God tells you that He created man in His image. In other words, He created you to be like Him. Since God is Spirit, He did not make you like Him physically; this must mean that He made you to be like Him spiritually. He is a God of love; and therefore, He has created you to love. When you love God and your neighbor (the two great commandments) you are behaving according to the way you were created. You are content because you were created to function in love. On the other hand, when you put your focus on self and take your focus off serving the Lord and others, you will "lose your life." You

37

© BIBLICAL COUNSELING FOUNDATION

LESSON 6

BIBLICAL PRACTICE:
YOUR DAILY WALK WITH CHRIST

may feel good while things are going well, but you will not have peace and joy in every circumstance. Consider the following illustration:

> ***ILLUSTRATION:*** Suppose a locomotive had a personality and decided one day that life was too restrictive. As it traveled, the locomotive noticed that animals were roaming about the beautiful countryside. In comparison, it was restricted to traveling along two very rigid railroad tracks. It said to itself, "I want to be free from this boring life. I want to escape from these tracks and travel through the countryside like those animals."
>
> Suppose that the locomotive were able to leave the tracks. What would happen?
>
> 6. _____
>
> Rather than being free, it would soon not be able to move at all. The point is that the locomotive was designed to function most efficiently when it was restricted to the tracks. In the same way, we function best as God intended and are completely fulfilled only when we die to self and serve God and others.

2. Let's look at a parallel passage to *Luke 9:24* to see another way that Jesus explained this truth. Read *John 12:24.* What does Jesus compare our lives to?

   7. _____

   Imagine a grain of wheat lying in a storage bin. It is dry and warm and comfortable with many other grains of wheat to keep it company, but it is not fulfilling its purpose. Not until it is placed in the cold, dark, damp ground without other grains nearby to keep it company, and not until it dies does it bear fruit and multiply.

   Now read *John 12:25.* Jesus is not just talking about grains of wheat. What is He talking about?

   8. _____

   In other words, He is pointing out how important it is not to be preoccupied with self but, instead, to focus our attention on the Lord and others.

   These truths are life-changing. Just think, if you truly were to die to self, nothing could hurt you. When you say that someone has hurt you, you really mean, "I am angry and bitter about what happened to me, and I don't like it." A dead body cannot be hurt. It is when you die daily that you can have contentment in the midst of even the most difficult circumstances.

B. The daily walk in Christ

   Living victoriously in the battles of life involves a moment-by-moment application of the principles of love, in the power of the Holy Spirit. It is based on taking the focus off yourself and consistently demonstrating your love for God and your neighbor.

© BIBLICAL COUNSELING FOUNDATION

LESSON 6

BIBLICAL PRACTICE:
YOUR DAILY WALK WITH CHRIST

As a soldier prepares for the physical battles, so a Christian must prepare for the daily spiritual battles of life. Your daily devotions (time spent each day in study of God's Word, biblical self-evaluation, and prayer) and Scripture memory are vital for you to learn to live consistently as a doer of the Word.

1. Devotions

   Read *Psalm 1:1-4*. Notice in *Psalm 1:2*, that a person is blessed if he does what?

   9. _____

   Meditation in the Scriptures is quite different from the meditation practiced by the secular world. The world encourages you to empty your mind and let it drift into areas that ignore life as it is. Biblical meditation is just the opposite. In *II Corinthians 10:5*, what does God tell you to do?

   10. _____

   Daily devotions should be times that help you learn to be *devoted* to the Lord. Many believers, knowing only that they should "have daily devotions," primarily rely on devotional books with Scripture passages for each day. These may be good and may lead you to great times of fellowship with and worship of the Lord. However, sometimes the devotional study applies to the current circumstances and sometimes it does not. It is important to recognize that devotional time spent in God's Word should also relate directly to the very areas in your life where God has your attention. Most often trials, relationships, and responsibilities are where your attention is already turned.

   Here is a suggested plan for conducting devotions in a way that applies to your current circumstances:

   a. Devotional study time
      1) Start by taking the log out of your own eye *(Matthew 7:1-5)*. Using *I Corinthians 13:4-8a* as a guide, prayerfully list ways in which you have failed to love biblically or have fallen to temptation. You may wish to start with one of the failures you have already listed on Page 32 in Question 5 of Lesson 5.
      2) Find Scripture passages that contain both "put-offs" and "put-ons" relating to the failures you just listed.
         a) To get started, you can use a concordance (a book that helps you find specific words in the Bible) or use the search feature on electronic Bibles. You may even have a concordance in the back of your Bible. Find a word or words that relate to your problem area. Then, select a particular passage that contains both "put-offs" and "put-ons." ***NOTE:*** *You may wish to review the teaching on "put-offs" and "put-ons" in Lesson 5.*
         b) Refer to Supplement 1 in this booklet on Page 43, titled "**Where to Find Biblical References to Specific Problem Areas**."
            i. You may find the list of Scripture passages at the top of Supplement 1 very useful in locating passages that are associated with the failures you have identified in Subparagraph 1).

© BIBLICAL COUNSELING FOUNDATION

LESSON 6

BIBLICAL PRACTICE:
YOUR DAILY WALK WITH CHRIST

   ii. If you have access to a **Self-Confrontation** manual (a Bible study book
        published by the Biblical Counseling Foundation), the chapters referenced
        next to each problem area may provide Scripture references related to the
        problem area you have chosen.

3) Make a plan to help you put off the particular sin pattern that you need to change
    and to put on the appropriate biblical pattern of righteousness to be established.

    a) See the **BIBLE STUDY AND APPLICATION FORMAT** shown below as an example
        using *Psalm 1:1-2.* This format is a useful aid to studying the Word of God with
        a view toward application to your own life. Notice that the format is based on
        II Timothy 3:16-17, which says that the Word of God is profitable for teaching,
        reproof, correction, and training in righteousness, that you might be thoroughly
        equipped to do what God wants you to do.

EXERCISE: BIBLE STUDY AND APPLICATION FORMAT FOR *PSALM 1:1-2*

As an exercise, complete the following questions from the **BIBLE STUDY AND APPLICATION
FORMAT** for *Psalm 1:1-2.* Use the following space to record your thoughts on these verses.

Teaching — What is the commandment or principle?

11. _____

Reproof — What do I need to lay aside or put off?

12. _____

_____

Correction — What do I need to start doing or put on?

13. _____

_____

Training in Righteousness — What is my specific plan? *(How* will I do what God commands
me to do?)

14. _____

_____

---

    b) Complete a **BIBLE STUDY AND APPLICATION FORMAT** for the Scripture passage
        you selected in 1. a. 2) above. You may wish to use the form at Supplement 2.

  b. Devotional prayer time

    1) Pray about what you just studied and acknowledge your dependence upon the Lord
        for wisdom, understanding of the Word, and strength to apply what you learned.

    2) Thank God for your circumstances.

    3) Confess all known sins to the Lord and ask for His help to overcome any sinful
        patterns that you recognize in your life.

© BIBLICAL COUNSELING FOUNDATION

LESSON 6

BIBLICAL PRACTICE:
YOUR DAILY WALK WITH CHRIST

2. Scripture memory

Read *Psalm 119:9, 11.* What benefits are there to treasuring God's Word in your heart and obeying it completely?

15. _____

It is important for you to have a specific plan for memorizing God's Word, starting with the verses that apply directy to your life in your current trials, tests, and temptations. From the list you develop during your devotional time, memorize at least one new Scripture verse a week and daily review the verses you have already learned.

It is best to memorize at times other than during your devotional time. Take advantage of "free" moments during the day to review memory verses. You will be making wise use of the "empty" times when temptations often arise due to undisciplined thinking. What types of free moments can you think of that are possibilities for you?

16. _____

_____

Be sure to write your memory verses on cards and carry them with you throughout the day.

In order to meditate on God's Word throughout the day, it is helpful to have a devotional time in the morning to start your day in the way the Lord wants you to live. Then, memorize and review your Scripture verses throughout the day to help you keep your mind focused on God's Word.

Then, a short devotional time in the evening helps you to review the day before the Lord, allowing you to judge yourself in light of God's standards and to make changes in your practices of life out of your commitment of loving obedience to Him.

C. What was the most significant truth you learned in completing this lesson?

17. _____

_____

D. What next?

If you would like more in-depth understanding of how to live victoriously, the Self-Confrontation course is essential. The course expands on all of these and many other principles, applies them to specific problem areas, and provides tools for application of the principles to your own circumstances.

The Self-Confrontation course is designed with two purposes in mind:

1) To help you experience victory and contentment in all of life's trials and problems by approaching relationships and circumstances from a biblical perspective, and

2) To prepare you to help others face, deal with, and endure their problems biblically.

In addition to covering the topics in this booklet in greater depth, the Self-Confrontation course deals with biblical principles relating to specific problem areas such as: anger and bitterness, forgiveness and reconciliation, biblical communication, marriage relationships, parent-child

© BIBLICAL COUNSELING FOUNDATION

LESSON 6

BIBLICAL PRACTICE:
YOUR DAILY WALK WITH CHRIST

relationships, depression, fear and worry, preoccupation with self, and life-dominating practices of sin.

The Self-Confrontation course can be conducted in several ways:

- **In your own personal devotions and Bible study** — For this choice, you may wish to use the *Student Workbook* along with the *Self-Confrontation* manual. The *Self-Confrontation* manual is the primary reference work for the course, and is designed to be a continuing reference for facing, dealing with, and enduring all problems of life. The *Student Workbook* is designed to lead you through a personal life-application study of God's Word, using the *Self-Confrontation* manual as a reference. It includes detailed explanations, exercises, and illustrations for each of the lessons in the manual.

- **As a small group Bible study on a weekly basis** — A DVD set is available for conducting the Self-Confrontation course in a small group setting. The *Self-Confrontation Bible Study Leader's Guide* provides a person having very little training with the capability to lead the small group very effectively.

- **As a regular class conducted once a week by an instructor** — The *Level 1 Instructor's Guide: Weekly* provides specific instructions for each of the 24 lessons of the Self-Confrontation course. It includes detailed explanations, exercises, and illustrations for each of the two-hour lessons. You can also use either the *Self-Confrontation DVD Series* or the *Self-Confrontation Audio Series* as a substitute for the instructor. It is best for the students to use the *Student Workbook* to complete their homework after each lesson rather than the homework provided at the end of each lesson in the *Self-Confrontation* manual.

- **As an intensive five-day course conducted by the Biblical Counseling Foundation** — This is a course conducted in various locations worldwide based on the invitation of various churches and other organizations to come to their area/country. The course is typically conducted Monday through Friday from 8:30 a.m. to 5:30 p.m. The schedule for all BCF courses is posted in advance on the BCF website: bcfmininistries.org.

- **As two Weekend Seminars conducted by the Biblical Counseling Foundation** — These courses are also conducted by invitation in various locations worldwide. Each seminar covers half of the Self-Confrontation course and can also be conducted on successive weekends in conjunction with other intensive BCF courses, which are conducted during the week between the Weekend Seminars. Sometimes, churches choose to host only the first Weekend Seminar initially and then host the second seminar later based on the attendance and results of the first seminar. Each seminar is conducted Friday evening, all day Saturday, and Sunday afternoon so that the local attendees do not need to miss any work or Sunday church activities.

The *Self-Confrontation* manual, the accompanying *Student Workbook*, and other related materials may be obtained from the Biblical Counseling Foundation. See the contact information on the inside cover of this booklet.

SUPPLEMENT 1

WHERE TO FIND BIBLICAL REFERENCES
TO SPECIFIC PROBLEM AREAS

Some key passages of Scripture to help with possible problem areas:

Proverbs Chapters 15 and 18
Romans Chapters 12 - 14
I Corinthians 13:4-8a
Ephesians 4:22 - 6:9
Colossians Chapter 3
I Peter 2:11 - 3:17

A sample set of problem areas:

Scripture references containing biblical principles, "put-offs," and "put-ons" for these problem areas can be found in the indicated lessons of the **Self-Confrontation** manual. In some of the referenced lessons, the problem area may not be specifically listed, but the biblical principles and biblical references will apply.

Anger — Lesson 11
Bitterness — Lesson 11
Communication, sinful (lying, slander, arguing, cursing) — Lesson 13
Contentment, lack of — Lesson 6
Envy, jealousy, covetousness, greed — Lessons 9 and 10
Depression (despair, lack of fulfilment of responsibilities, total inactivity) — Lesson 18
Drug abuse — Lessons 20 and 21
Drunkenness — Lessons 20 and 21
Eating problems (overeating; starving self, called "anorexia;" or binging on food and purging self, called "bulimia") — Lessons 9, 10, 20, and 21
Fear (including "panic attacks") — Lesson 19
Gambling — Lessons 20 and 21
Grief focused on self — Lessons 9, 10, 20 and 21
Lust — Lessons 9, 10, 20-21
Marriage problems — Lessons 14 and 15
Parent-child problems — Lessons 16 and 17
Reconciliation problems — Lessons 12 and 13
Relationship problems (marriage, relative, acquaintances, etc.) — Lessons 12-17, 20 and 21
Satanic influences — Lessons 20 and 21
Self-belittlement — Lessons 9 and 10
Self-exaltation — Lessons 9 and 10
Self-pity — Lessons 9 and 10
Sexual sins (adultery, fornication, homosexuality, pornography) — Lessons 20 and 21
Stealing (covetousness) — Lessons 9 and 10
Stewardship problems (body, time, material goods, abilities) — Lesson 10
Unforgiveness — Lesson 12
Worry (anxiety) — Lesson 19

© BIBLICAL COUNSELING FOUNDATION

44

© BIBLICAL COUNSELING FOUNDATION

SUPPLEMENT 2

BIBLE STUDY AND APPLICATION FORMAT

BIBLE STUDY AND APPLICATION FORMAT

Sin pattern that I need to change

Biblical Reference

Teaching — What is the commandment or principle?

Reproof — What do I need to lay aside or put-off?

Correction — What do I need to start doing or put-on?

Training in Righteousness — What is my specific plan? *(How* will I do what God commands me to do?)

Permission is granted to reproduce this form for personal or ministry use. © BIBLICAL COUNSELING FOUNDATION

46

© BIBLICAL COUNSELING FOUNDATION

SUPPLEMENT 3

ANSWERS TO QUESTIONS IN THE BOOKLET

LESSON 1

1. The purpose of God's directing John to write down the events in his Gospel is **so that I may believe that Jesus is the Christ, the Son of God; and that believing I may have life in His name**.

2. The first part of *II Timothy 3:16* says of God's Word that **all Scripture is inspired by God**.

3. In *II Timothy 3:16,* the four things the Scriptures are profitable for are: **Teaching, reproof, correction, and training in righteousness**.

4. In *II Timothy 3:17,* the end result is **that the man of God may be adequate, equipped for all good works**.

5. According to *John 5:24,* my eternal life depends on **hearing the Word of Jesus Christ and believing the one who sent Him, God the Father**.

6. According to *Romans 6:23,* eternal life **is a free gift of God which is in Christ Jesus, our Lord**.

7. According to in *Ephesians 2:8-9,* **we are saved by grace through faith and that not of ourselves, it is the gift of God; not as a result of works, so that no one may boast**.

8. According to *John 14:26* and *John 16:13,* **The Holy Spirit will teach me all things, bring to my remembrance all that Jesus says to me, and guide me into all truth**.

9. According to *Romans 5:5,* **the Holy Spirit pours out the love of God within our hearts**.

10. According to *Psalm 116:1-2,* God **hears my voice and my supplications and He inclines His ear to me**.

11. According to *Psalm 66:18,* something that can get in the way of my communication with God is **if I regard wickedness in my heart, The Lord will not hear me**.

12. To restore our fellowship with God, God says we need to **confess our sins**.

13. God's promise if I confess my sins is that **He is faithful and righteous to forgive me and to cleanse me from all unrighteousness**.

14. In *I Corinthians 12:26,* God says that as members of the body of Christ, **if one member suffers, I suffer with that member; if one member is honored, I rejoice with that member**.

15. According to *Hebrews 10:24-25,* some of the things God says we should be doing with others in the body of Christ are **to stimulate one another to love and good deeds, not forsake assembling together with other believers, and encourage one another**.

16. According to *Romans 12:2,* we are not to be **conformed** to the world.

17. According to *Romans 12:2* we are to be **transformed** by the renewing of our mind.

18. According to *Psalm 119:9, 11,* the benefits to treasuring God's Word in my heart and obeying it completely are that **it keeps my way pure and helps me not to sin**.

© BIBLICAL COUNSELING FOUNDATION

SUPPLEMENT 3

ANSWERS TO QUESTIONS IN THE BOOKLET

19. Answers will vary. Typical types of free moments may include: **waiting in line, waiting for appointments, riding on a bus or a train, etc.**

20. Answers will vary.

LESSON 2

1. The two parts to the command in *Matthew 28:19-20,* are **1) baptizing and 2) teaching them to observe all that He commanded**.

2. In *Ephesians 2:2,* **we used to walk according to the course of this world**.

3. According to *Ephesians 2:10,* **believers are created to do good works**.

4. In *Ephesians 2:4,* our motivation for good works should be that **we do good works because of God's great mercy and love for us**.

5. *Galatians 5:16* says that **if we walk by the Spirit, we will not carry out the desire of the flesh**.

6. Regarding our daily struggle with sin, God says in *Galatians 5:17* that **the flesh sets its desire against the Spirit, and the Spirit against the flesh; for these are in opposition to one another, so that we do not do the things we please**.

7. The characteristics of the fruit of the Spirit listed in *Galatians 5:22-23* are **love, joy, peace, patience, kindness, goodness, faithfulness, gentleness, and self-control**.

8. According to *I Peter 1:6-7,* **my faith bringing praise and glory and honor to Jesus Christ** is more precious than gold.

9. Regarding trials, in *I Peter 4:12-13,* God says that **we should not be surprised when trials come because they are for our testing**.

10. Answers will vary regarding any trials that you have been "surprised" by in your life.

11. According to *I Peter 4:12-13,* **I can rejoice at the revelation of His glory** through the trial in Question 10. above.

12. According to *James 1:13-14,* **God** is *not* the source of temptation.

13. According to *James 1:13-14,* **our own lust (fleshly desires)** *is* a source of temptation.

14. According to *I John 2:16,* the three areas of temptation listed are (a) **the lust of the flesh**, (b) **the lust of the eyes**, and (c) **the boastful pride of life**.

15. Answers will vary regarding examples of temptations in each of the categories in Question 14. above.

16. Answers will vary.

LESSON 3

1. In *Romans 1:18-20,* the issue of man's separation from God is not a matter of a lack of knowledge, but that **man rejects the truth that he is given**.

© BIBLICAL COUNSELING FOUNDATION

SUPPLEMENT 3

ANSWERS TO QUESTIONS IN THE BOOKLET

2. In *Romans 1:21-23,* when people reject God, the consequences in their lives are that **they think they are wise, but they become fools, their hearts are darkened. They begin to worship the creation instead of the Creator**.

3. In *Romans 1:32,* they sink to lowest depth **by giving hearty approval of those who do the same**.

4. The names of the three levels typed in **boldface** print on the chart on Page 21 are (a) **heart level**, (b) **doing level**, and (c) **feeling level**.

5. According to *Jeremiah 17:9-10,* **God** is the only one who is able to see a person's heart completely.

6. According to *Luke 5:22,* Jesus likens the heart to **the mind**.

7. The thoughts listed in *Matthew 15:18-19* are **evil thoughts**.

8. The speech listed in *Matthew 15:18-19* are **false witness, slanders**.

9. The actions listed in *Matthew 15:18-19* are **murders, adulteries, fornications, thefts**.

10. **Consistently doing the Word** is more difficult than understanding my position in Christ.

11. Answers will vary. Examples of situations in which a person may not have good feelings, and yet there is no sin involved would be: (a) **when a person is ill with the flu** or (b) **when a person is grieving the loss of a loved one**.

12. We know that feelings are not sin and that God does not hold us responsible for changing our feelings because **we are never commanded to change our feelings**.

13. Answers will vary; for example, **the motor is out of oil, the oil pump is out of commission, or the oil light is defective**.

14. The student's focus of attention as he went through the downward spiral was **on himself**.

15. Answers will vary.

LESSON 4

1. Pointing out that the one who is drunk is committing sin and is not doomed by an illness brings hope to a person because **he can confess sin, establish or restore a right relationship with God quickly, and be freed from the power of sin**.

2. In *Romans 6:18,* God says that **believers are slaves of righteousness**.

3. In *I Corinthians 10:13,* God says that temptations are **common to man**, that **God will not allow me to be tempted beyond what I am able to handle**, that **He will provide the way of escape**, and that **the way of escape is so that I may be able to endure the temptation**.

4. In *I Corinthians 10:13,* **my escape is not from the situation, but from sin so that I can endure the situation**.

5. Regarding trials, God says in *James 1:2-4* that **I should consider it joy when I encounter trials because these tests of faith produce endurance**.

6. In *Hebrews 12:2,* the joy set before Jesus was **sitting at the right hand of His Father**.

© BIBLICAL COUNSELING FOUNDATION

SUPPLEMENT 3

ANSWERS TO QUESTIONS IN THE BOOKLET

7. According to *Matthew 26:39,* **no**, Jesus did **not** enjoy going to the cross.

8. According to *Romans 8:29,* the "good" is for us to **be conformed to the image of God's Son, Jesus Christ**.

9. In *Genesis 37:23-28,* the trials and injustices that God allowed in Joseph's life were that **his brothers sold him into slavery**.

10. In *Genesis 39:11-20,* the trials and injustices that God allowed in Joseph's life were that **he was unjustly accused of adultery and put in prison**.

11. In *Genesis 40:12-14, 23,* the trials and injustices that God allowed in Joseph's life were that **the chief cupbearer forgot about him**.

12. The erroneous proverb in *Ezekiel 18:2* was: **when fathers eat sour grapes, the children's teeth are set on edge**.

13. In *Ezekiel 18:3-4,* God **tells the Israelites to get rid of that proverb. He holds each person responsible for his own behavior**.

14. Answers will vary. Some examples of sin reaping physical consequences to others not responsible for the sin include: (a) **a drunkard does not provide the nutritional food that the children need to be healthy** and (b) **a mother has contracted AIDS through sinful behavior and transmits the AIDS to her newborn child**.

15. The hope about problems offered in *I John 1:9* is that **if I confess my sins, God forgives me and cleanses me from all sin**.

16. Answers will vary.

LESSON 5

1. In *James 1:2-5,* God promises wisdom for **the trial I am going through**.

2. In *James 1:22,* God says that if I do not obey His Word, **I will delude myself**.

3. In *Hebrews 4:16,* God promises give me His grace **at the time of need**.

4. The two commandments Jesus states in *Matthew 22:37-40* are (a) **love God**, and (b) **love my neighbor as myself**.

5. Answers will vary regarding areas of love listed in *I Corinthians 13* that I have difficulty demonstrating.

6. According to *Matthew 7:5,* before dealing with anyone else's failures, **I am to take the log out of my own eye**.

7. If I listen to the teaching from Scripture but do not apply it in my own life, Jesus says **I am a hypocrite**.

8. According to *Matthew 7:5,* **after being able to see clearly, I am to help my brother take the speck out of his eye**.

9. The "put-off" in *Ephesians 4:25* is **falsehood**.

10. The "put-on" in *Ephesians 4:25* is **speaking truth**.

© BIBLICAL COUNSELING FOUNDATION

SUPPLEMENT 3

ANSWERS TO QUESTIONS IN THE BOOKLET

11. **Yes**, it is possible for someone to put off lying and never put on speaking the truth **by not saying anything**.

12. The "put-off" in *Ephesians 4:28* is **stealing**.

13. The "put-on" in *Ephesians 4:28* is **working and giving to those who have need**.

14. **No**, if a robber has stopped robbing after stealing a million dollars, it does not mean that he is no longer a robber. **He may just be busy spending the money that he has stolen**.

15. The "put-off" in *Ephesians 4:29* is **unwholesome words**.

16. The "put-on" in *Ephesians 4:29* is **edifying words that give grace according to the need of the moment**.

17. The "put-offs" in *Ephesians 4:31-32* are **bitterness, wrath, anger, clamor, slander, and malice**.

18. The "put-ons" in *Ephesians 4:31-32* are **kindness, tenderheartedness, and forgiveness**.

19. To help the student, I should deal with salvation first **because lack of salvation is his most significant problem, and I may mistakenly be helping him to feel better, and thus remove an incentive for him to seek God to be saved**.

20. Answers will vary.

LESSON 6

1. According to *Hebrews 5:12-14,* without the practice of God's Word, **I will not be able to discern between good and evil, i.e., I will not be wise**.

2. God says in *James 1:22* that if I am not a doer of the Word, **I will be in a worse spiritual state because I will delude myself**.

3. The cross is a symbol of **death**.

4. The "put-on" in *Luke 9:23-24* is to **follow Jesus**.

5. When I focus on finding my life, **I lose my life**.

6. If the locomotive was able to leave the tracks, **it would get stuck in the ground and would not be able to move**.

7. In *John 12:24,* Jesus compares our lives to **a grain of wheat**.

8. In *John 12:25,* Jesus is not just talking about grains of wheat, **He is talking about dying to self**.

9. In *Psalm 1:2,* a person is blessed if he **meditates in God's law day and night**.

10. In *II Corinthians 10:5,* God tells me to **take every thought captive to the obedience of Christ**.

11. The commandment or principle in *Psalm 1:2* is to **delight in the Law of the Lord and meditate on it constantly**.

12. Answers will vary regarding the reproof in *Psalm 1:2.* A typical response might be: "**I don't meditate on the Word consistently**."

© BIBLICAL COUNSELING FOUNDATION

SUPPLEMENT 3

ANSWERS TO QUESTIONS IN THE BOOKLET

13. Answers will vary regarding the correction in *Psalm 1:2.* A typical response might be: "**I need to have His Word in my mind much more throughout the day.**"

14. Answers will vary regarding the training in righteousness based on *Psalm 1:2.* A typical response might be: "**I will carry my Scripture memory cards with me and review them during the spare moments of each day.**"

15. In *Psalm 119:9, 11,* the benefits to treasuring God's Word in my heart and obeying it completely are that **it keeps my way pure and helps me not to sin**.

16. Answers will vary. Typical types of free moments may include: **waiting in line, waiting for appointments, riding on a bus or a train, etc.**

17. Answers will vary.

© BIBLICAL COUNSELING FOUNDATION